I0829152

THE PRO RATA QUESTION.

REMARKS

OF

J. W. BROOKS, Esq.,

BEFORE THE

COMMITTEES ON RAILROADS

OF THE

SENATE AND ASSEMBLY OF THE STATE OF NEW YORK,

March 30th, 1869.

ALBANY:
WEED, PARSONS AND COMPANY, PRINTERS.
1869.

THE

PRO RATA QUESTION.

Mr. BROOKS said:

Mr. Chairman and Gentlemen of the Committee:

It is not long since the State of New York owned the only really effective freight-carrying avenue between the food-producing regions of the west and the Atlantic seaboard.

The early opening of the Erie canal to the lakes at once put the country about these waters ahead of all the west in settlement, population and business.

The canals and early railroads of that country were all built, from the lakes to the interior, to drain the traffic towards the only avenue to market.

New States grew up, and business multiplied beyond precedent at the sources of this outlet, and the vast wealth and trade of an immense country became tributary solely to the city of New York.

This, and the construction of her railroads before that of the more southern lines, has made New York what it is.

New lines of railroad have now been built from other Atlantic cities whose branches and connections have covered the whole west with a net-work of railroads, destroying all monopolies, and opening the business equally to all comers.

These new lines have, within a very short time, perfected their tracks and greatly improved and enlarged their facilities for doing business, while many new lines are being built which point to them as their trunk-lines to market.

In this condition of things it becomes every thinking man who wishes well to New York, and has the power to affect her weal or woe, to do all he can to strengthen her hold upon the sources of her prosperity.

Every thing should be done to increase the power of her railroads to compete with rival lines for the carrying trade of the west that they may bring her business to New York; and nothing should be done to restrain the freest exercise of that power, if restraining it will, as I apprehend, render it less effective.

The geographical position of New York, in respect to this traffic, is such as to render it quite clear that her prosperity is not due to her position, but solely to her early enterprise in opening avenues of transit to the west ahead of her neighbors.

In respect to carriage by rail, which we are now considering, the State of Pennsylvania lies between the city of New York and the west, and Lake Erie lies between the State and the west. Freight, therefore, from the city through this State to the west, has to be carried a long way to the north, then across the State to the shore of Lake Erie, then south to get round the lakes, until it gets back again as far south as the city of New York, before it arrives at the point attained by the more southern lines, on their routes directly west from the seaboard.

To permanently retain a fair share of the carrying trade over such comparatively roundabout routes, will require the utmost economy, the wisest foresight, and the freest ability to cope with the perplexities, obstacles and difficulties which daily arise, in a business of such extensive ramifications and multifarious interests.

It never could have been more wisely said, that "eternal vigilance is the price of success."

There are several centers in the western States, where a considerable portion of the business originates, or through which it passes.

The order in which these are geographically situated, most favorable to the New York Central Road, are somewhat as follows:

1st. *Detroit*, through which passes most of the traffic of the State of Michigan, including that of Lake Superior.

2d. *Cleveland*, through which passes the business of the northern portion of Ohio, the most of Indiana, the southerly half of Illinois, a portion of north Missouri and of southern Iowa.

3d. *Chicago*, to which converges the business of the northern part of Illinois, Wisconsin, Minnesota, part of Iowa and a part of north Missouri.

4th. *St. Louis*, through which passes a large portion of the business of Missouri, a portion of Kansas, and much of the lower Mississippi valley generally.

5th. *Cincinnati*, through which passes much of the business of the southern part of Ohio, the Ohio valley below Cincinnati, and a portion of the business of the lower Mississippi valley.

Of these several centers, Chicago, Cincinnati and St. Louis, are many times the largest, and have rapidly increasing areas of territory tributary to them; while Detroit and Cleveland are comparatively small, and not capable of such increasing expansion.

The distances of these various points, through which the business of the respective districts is drained, to New York, are as follows:

I.—DETROIT TO NEW YORK:

	Miles.	Miles longer than Shortest Route.
1. Via Canada and New York Central,	677	
2. " Toledo, Cleveland and Penn. Central,	758	81
3. " Toledo, Cleveland and New York and Erie,	780	103
4. " Toledo, Cleveland and Baltimore and Ohio,	880	~~113~~ 203

II.—CLEVELAND TO NEW YORK:

	Miles.	Miles longer than Shortest Route.
1. Via Pittsburgh and Penn. Central,	581	
2. " Lake Shore and New York and Erie,	603	22
3. " Lake Shore and New York Central,	625	44
4. " Pittsburgh, Wheeling and Baltimore and Ohio,	703	122

III.—CHICAGO TO NEW YORK:

	Miles.	Miles longer than Shortest Route.
1. Via Fort Wayne and Penn. Central,	899	
2. " Lake Shore and New York and Erie,	958	59
3. " Detroit, Canada and New York Central,	960	61
4. " Logansport and Baltimore and Ohio,	1016	117

IV.—St. Louis to New York:

	Route	Miles	Difference
1.	Via Indianapolis and Penn. Central,.... ..1074	1074	
2.	" Cincinnati and Baltimore and Ohio,.....	1113	39
3.	" Indianapolis, Cleveland and New York and Erie,........................	1148	74
4.	" Indianapolis, Cleveland and New York Central, ...	1170	96

V.—Cincinnati to New York:

	Route	Miles	Difference
1.	Via Columbus, Pittsburgh and Penn. Central,	744	
2.	" Parkersburg and Baltimore and Ohio,...	774	30
3.	" Cleveland and New York and Erie,.....	861	117
4.	" Cleveland and New York Central,......	883	139

From these tables it is clear that if the traffic which has made the city of New York is still to pass through the State, it must be carried by her railroads at a *less* rate per mile than if carried by their competitors at the South, for much bitter and expensive experience has settled the principle that the rates between all competing points must be alike over all the routes, which would share in the carrying trade, irrespective of their length.

As no two of these routes are of the same length, the prices charged upon any articles of freight between two competing points must be at a different rate per mile upon each of the routes—less per mile upon the longer, and more per mile upon the shorter line.

From Chicago to New York, by the shortest route, in connection with the New York Central Road, is 960 miles; by the Baltimore and Ohio it is 1016 miles. The former would get about 6 per cent more per mile than the latter for the same business.

From Cincinnati to New York, by the shortest route in connection with the New York Central Road, is 833 miles; the same via Pittsburgh and Philadelphia, is 744 miles. The former must, consequently, carry for about 19 per cent less per mile than the latter.

Each road will, therefore, get more per mile upon some of its long traffic than its rival lines, and less upon other of its long traffic.

It has been found in practice, that the only equitable, as well as practicable method of dividing the price received for the transportation of freight between competing points, over a route composed of several separate roads, is, by the distance carried upon each road, a pro rata per mile, with such moderate allowances for ferries, &c., as may be equitable to the parties who support them for the common benefit. .

Any road which would not recognize this principle, and should insist upon a uniform rate upon freight from all sources, would soon lose a large portion of its long traffic. If, for example, the New York Central would not take its pro rata portion of the through rates with the roads west and south of Cleveland, those lines would send their business from all of Ohio, Kentucky, Indiana, Illinois, Wisconsin, Iowa, Minnesota, Missouri, in fact the business of the whole of the Ohio and Mississippi valley, by the more southern routes to New York. Any other plan of division would take from one road a portion of its earnings to give to another. It inevitably results, that every line participating in the long business must carry the same kinds of freight at different rates of charges, when coming from different competing points, at lower rates when the road forms a part of the longer line, and at higher rates when it forms part of the shorter line between the competing points.

From St. Louis to the west end of the State of New York, there are many routes through which the traffic of that city flows. The five principal ones are:

1st. Via Chicago, through Canada.

2d. Via Chicago and the south shore of Lake Erie.

3d. Via the Wabash Valley line to Toledo, and thence by the Lake Shore.

4th. Via Indianapolis and Crestline to Cleveland, and thence by the Lake Shore.

5th. Via Cincinnati to Cleveland, and thence by the Lake Shore.

Now, as these routes are all of different lengths, and must work for the same through rates, some will get more, and some less, per mile for the same kind of freight. Suppose one of the New York roads demurs at the rate, and, for some reason or peculiar position of its own, asks more? Who is to pay that more? It belongs to the roads which have earned it, and what belongs to one road is not likely to be paid to another.

There is, really, no question as to what is to be done. Nobody is required to pay more; nobody is interested to pay more; the traffic is at once thrown over another line to market.

It is a matter of no consequence to the owner of the goods, or to the road near to St. Louis, which originates and directs the freight, what route it takes to market.

It is simply a question of rate; and, what affects the route of traffic from St. Louis, will affect it from the hundreds of other competing points. Like causes will produce like results.

Of the some 2,000 miles of railroads, with which I am connected, in the States of Michigan, Indiana, Illinois, Iowa, Missouri and Kansas, whose arms and branches cover a front, stretching from Omaha, about 400 miles southward, to near Arkansas, there is but one, with which it is not a matter of perfect indifference whether their traffic goes through the State of New York, or otherwise to market.

It may be suggested, that the through rates are lower than is necessary; this may well be left to those whose daily business is but a continued experience, qualifying them as judges in this matter. Except in cases of unsettled competition, when the public gets all the advantage, the interest of the companies will lead them to procure as high rates as the business will bear.

By the natural laws of trade, the shortest route between competing points, exercises the most influence in fixing the rates, and when the difference is very great, the shortest line controls it. In other words, *whatever the shortest route is willing to take the traffic for, the longer routes must accept, or get no traffic.*

The New York roads, therefore, being much the longest, exercise the least influence, and upon the largest portion of the long traffic can have no influence whatever to keep up the rates.

Before the great increase of railroads in the Western States, the business of each district of that great region had but one general way to get to and from a market. The trade of the Ohio and Mississippi valleys proper went via New Orleans, and that of the lakes by the Erie canal. Rates of freight could then be changed without so sensibly affecting the course of the traffic, and without very materially reducing the area drained in any particular direction. Moderate changes would, in those days, rather have affected the production, than changed the current of traffic. The multitude of railroads which now lattice the Western States have rendered all the natural, as well as the artificial channels of trade, accessible throughout every part of that region.

Facilities for transportation have increased upon all the outlets for Western freight, methods of management have been simplified, the cost reduced, certainty, dispatch and safety very much enhanced, in efforts to take business via New Orleans,—not only upon the Ohio and Mississippi, but as well upon the northern artificial avenues to the seaboard.

If the rate of freight between St. Louis and New York be raised but a little too high, a large proportion of it will go via New Orleans; and that requiring a more speedy route to market will take the river via Cincinnati and Wheeling, reaching the seaboard by the Baltimore and Ohio and Pennsylvania Central roads. The same may be said of the rate from Cincinnati; and whatever changes the route of freight from these points, will also change that of two-thirds of the whole West, and other kindred causes will alike affect the rest. It is, therefore, wholly out of the power of the railroad lines to control the price of the long freight; they must take it at the rates at which it is moving through other channels, or lose it altogether.

The margin for profit upon all produce transactions and mercantile business generally, in the Western States, has been reduced by the extended use of the magnetic telegraph and the increased facilities for transportation, thereby rendering all holders of property for transportation very sensitive to small changes in the rates, which would not, in years past, have been noticed. These and other causes have rendered the tenure, by which the East and West lines hold a portion of the traffic of the West, such as to require constant and watchful care. A very moderate increase of rates, especially while the Ohio and Mississippi are free from ice, would largely reduce the area of country drained to the eastward.

It may be urged, that as the trade of the West can reach New York as well by the more southern routes, as those of New York State, the experiment of a light toll might be put upon the latter without proving eminently hazardous to the western business.

The answer to this would be, that, although the other lines are as short, and in many cases much shorter, to New York, than the New York routes, yet they are controlled and managed by an interest wholly adverse to that of the State of New York.

With all these avenues opened from rival cities to the source of trade which has created New York, her every effort should be exerted to add to and not reduce her facilities for trade with the West. Is it wise for New York to be indebted to rival interests for her trade with the West? Is it prudent to allow her traffic to pass through rival cities before reaching her?

It is well worth while to inquire into the relative distances between the great centers of western trade and the cities of New York, Philadelphia and Baltimore. They are as follows:

	Miles.	Nearer than to New York.
From Detroit to New York, ...	677	
From Detroit to Philadelphia, ...	614	63
From Detroit to Baltimore,....................	703	26
From Cleveland to New York,.................	603	
From Cleveland to Philadelphia, ...	505	98
From Cleveland to Baltimore, ...	517	86
From Chicago to New York, ...	958	
From Chicago to Philadelphia,.................	823	135
From Chicago to Baltimore, ...	802	156
From St. Louis to New York,..................	1074	
From St. Louis to Philadelphia,................	998	76
From St. Louis to Baltimore, ...	927	147
From Cincinnati to New York,................	744	
From Cincinnati to Philadelphia,..............	663	81
From Cincinnati to Baltimore, ...	586	158

A line drawn due south from Dunkirk across the Pennsylvania Central and Baltimore and Ohio railroads, as shown in the map herewith, will be distant from New York, by the New York Central and Hudson River roads, 482 miles; and by the Erie road, 460 miles; while the same line will be distant from Philadelphia, by the Pennsylvania Central road, but 322 miles; and from Baltimore, by the Baltimore and Ohio road, only 234 miles. This line is thus 160 miles nearer Philadelphia than New York by the New York Central, and 248 miles nearer Baltimore.

The distance from Baltimore, westward to this north and south line, is less than half the distance from New York by the Central road.

From this, and the foregoing table of distances, it appears that very large portions of the west are much nearer to Philadelphia and to Baltimore than to New York by the New York roads, and some of the most wealthy and prosperous districts are more than 200 miles nearer.

It has been said that the higher grades of these more southern roads make them, comparatively, longer than their miles would indicate. They run directly through the coal fields, and their cheaper fuel probably more than makes up the difference in grades.

The merchants of our large western cities are beginning to import quite largely on their own account. Competition and rivalry among them will soon make this the rule rather than the exception. These imports will, of course, be directed to that city which is nearest the west in respect to the cost of transportation.

Already nearly all the West is supplied with coffee imported through Baltimore, and even New York city has to go there for much of its supplies. The comparative nearness of that city to the West has given them a most significant monopoly of this very large trade.

In view of the fact that the western importer is likely to make his home purchases in the city where his imports arrive, it is of eminent importance to New York that the passage of their imports through her city should be retained. This clearly cannot be done excepting the rate of freight to the West be as low as from the other cities.

These more southern cities are but just entering upon the advantages of their position. Want of communication has heretofore excluded them from participating in a trade built up, and, until now, monopolized by New York.

Philadelphia's population has increased to nearly three-quarters of a million, and these advantages are but just opened to her; with their development her progress will certainly be greatly accelerated.

Both the Pennsylvania Central and Baltimore and Ohio railroads, were built from motives of State and city policy. A profitable investment for capital was not the moving cause for the construction of either; they were constructed for the promotion of the interests of their respective States and the cities where they terminate. Their destiny cannot be fulfilled, excepting by taking to their cities a large share of the trade of the West.

The means of defense possessed by New York, to counteract the effect produced by these new rivals for a trade heretofore her own, are simply the New York Central and New York and Erie railroads. If there is a way by which these lines can better facilitate the long traffic, or by which it can be done at a still more moderate rate of compensation, it is greatly for the interest of the State of New York that such a method should be devised. The canal can carry the heavy goods, but the freight which goes by rail will find its way over some one of the railway lines. It is therefore for the interest of New York to enable her roads to carry all freight which the most liberal policy and well devised system can obtain, and as the rate is the prime moving cause to direct the current, every possible accommodation should be given to business from competing points, and the most liberal policy towards the New York roads is absolutely essential to enable them to do and retain this business. Not only does much of the present trade of New York with the West depend upon this, but also that of all its future increase.

It has been suggested that it was unfair to charge rates for local business materially higher for the distances carried than those for through business. A little consideration will exhibit the fallacy of this view.

The construction of a railroad, through any section of a State, gives to that section peculiar advantages, the value of which is many times that of any return it can make to the railroad.

By its construction, and its vast and expensive equipment, it provides an avenue to market which is both regular and certain as well as cheap and expeditious.

The money invested to produce this beneficial result rarely pays so high a rate of interest as that invested in other property, and much of it never pays anything.

While their construction confers such vast benefits upon the localities they traverse, the good which any single road does, at a competing point, is comparatively small.

The rates from St. Louis, for instance, are largely controlled by the price of water carriages, the railroads really reducing the rates but very little.

At inland competing points, the tendency of a new line is rather to divide the business than reduce the rate. The great and positive benefits are largely local to the people living on the line.

The simple question bearing upon the rate for local charges should be, are they in amount just and proper? They most certainly are, if about equal to the usual charge of other railroads, and will then no more than yield a fair income upon the capital invested in the enterprise. It is neither wrong nor unjust to the people along the line that the foreign traffic should be done at lower rates, provided that it is not done at less than cost. In the latter case the company would be rendered less able to do the local business at a fair rate, but, as long as the through business paid any profit at all, it would, to just the extent of that profit, render the company able to modify its local charges, and still act justly as trustees to its stockholders.

All thinking men concede that unprofitable railroads do not satisfactorily respond to the just expectation of their patrons. It is for the interest of all parties that every enterprise of public utility should be remunerative to those who engage in it, and especially is it for the interest of the community, directly reaping the advantages of a good, safe, well-managed railroad, or rather reaping the inconveniences and discomfort of an unsafe, unreliable one for the transaction of their daily business.

These positions being true, it is for the interest of all concerned that the New York road should do all the through business it can procure, from which any profit can be gleaned, even if the rate be very low indeed.

The cost of doing contingent business is not as great as that of the original or fixed business; there are certain very large expenses not influenced by the amount of business, such as the decay of all perishable materials in the track, bridges, stations, cars, wash of banks and roadway, damages by fire and flood, and a great variety of expenditures which, in the aggregate, would probably amount to one-third of the whole. The expenses which should be regarded as properly attachable to any new business, procured from abroad by competition, are but about two-thirds as much as those chargeable to the business already done. With this just view of the cost of new business, as compared with that already being performed, it is clear that new business can be sought at pretty low rates and still yield a profit.

I have said that parties interested in the local business should not complain unless the long business should be done at less than cost, and the company thus be rendered less able to do the local business at a fair rate. There may be exceptional cases; if, from any causes of competition, connected with the foreign traffic, the road is liable to lose its hold upon that traffic, it is for the local interest that every method should be taken to retain it, even should it be carried for a time below cost. Better suffer this for a time than risk the permanent loss of a profitable business.

It is easy to see that a law attempting to establish a relation between the through and local rates would be most injurious to the city and State of New York, and the local patrons of the Central line, as well as to the railroad itself. The two classes of business are so radically different, that establishing any such relation would be destructive to all interests.

When the subject is fairly understood it will be seen that perfect harmony of all interests is found, in giving to the roads that unembarrassed freedom to compete for the through business, which will enable them to bring the largest possible amount of it through the State.

It frequently happens that a scarcity of cotton at New Orleans, with which to load foreign ships, or a violent competition on the Ohio and Mississippi rivers, will cause a temporary drainage of freight in that direction, from the territory usually drained eastward to New York.

A sudden fall of breadstuffs in New York will often have the same effect of checking the flow eastward.

Under such circumstances a reduction of rates is the only way to keep up the current of traffic.

In practice, this subject is brought up by the question whether the cars bringing out merchandise to this region shall be sent back empty, or loaded at reduced rates.

The ordinary rate from St. Louis to New York is, say $1.75 per barrel, or $3,500 per train of twenty car loads, which it costs, say $2,500 to take through. All that can be got for freight is $1.10 per barrel, or $2,200 for the train load. This is below cost, and will involve a loss of $300, but as it will cost $2,000 to take back the empty train, loading it at $300 less than the cost of transportation will result in a saving of $1,700.

Now, suppose the New York Central declines to take the rates, because it will cause a reduction in the rates on their local traffic. The reply, that this has nothing to do with local business, is met by the rejoinder, that this matter is not one to be governed by business principles or individual judgment, but of law. It cannot be discussed or arranged. They decline the freight.

Nothing remains to be said. The New York agents of the St. Louis roads are directed to send their westward freight through Philadelphia, and permanent arrangements are at once made with a line, that won't break down, every time the wind blows, ~~and~~ for a day or week ~~work~~ unfavorably.

The New York Central may attempt to fight alone in New York, the battle for westward freight, but what are they to do with it, if they get any? Nobody wants it, for nobody can afford to take it through and bring the cars back empty; the westward rate won't pay for working the trains both ways, and so the New York Central road is thrown out of the long traffic altogether, simply because they are not free to do business, upon business principles, and meet, in a business way, the exigencies that daily arise in the traffic. This company must hereafter look to their local business alone to work the road, keep up the property and pay a fair interest upon its capital, which clearly cannot be done at the present local rates. They must be raised, or the character and standing of the railroad will deteriorate.

In so far as the local rates of the New York Central are dependent upon the rates they receive from the long traffic from other roads, just so far will their ability to obtain such foreign traffic be destroyed. If this dependence be applied to but a few articles, those few will cease to be carried by them in the long traffic. If it applies to all kinds of freight, they will be forced out of the long traffic entirely.

A little illustration will make this clear. Suppose one of two rival merchants, selling dry goods and groceries in the same town, agrees with his customers that if he makes any reduction in the price of his dry goods, he will make the same relative reduction in the price of his groceries. His rival learns of it, and at once reduces the price of his dry goods, the other cannot follow, because the reduction on his whole business will ruin him. As he cannot sell the dry goods higher than his neighbor, he is forced to give up that part of his trade. His rival, having the whole market, sells twice as much, makes up for the reduction, and secures the good will of the public.

This seems a perfect parallel to our case.

If the Pennsylvania Central road could not reduce the rates upon its long traffic, without reducing those upon its local, it is clear that the other lines would find it for their interest to follow the example of the merchant, and dispossess that company of its share in the long traffic.

I once had a case quite in point. The Michigan Central railroad and their steamboat connection, between Cleveland and Detroit, formed a route between Cleveland and Chicago, which at one time excited the jealousy of the all rail route, between Cleveland and Chicago via Toledo. The all rail route insisted that we should charge the same rate that they did; whereas we had charged less, according to the custom of part water routes. They took off the dollar difference, and began to follow our price, when I gave orders to our agent to let them fix the rate, and charge one dollar less by our route. Now, as their business was then, nearly all through from Cleveland, nine-tenths of their traffic was exposed to the fire, and not one-tenth of ours. The dollar difference was agreed to, and the whole matter settled itself as quickly as a strife between the New York Central and the Pennsylvania Central would settle itself, if the former was so hampered, from any cause, that it could not compete with the latter on equal terms. It would be like a man in the stocks, fighting with a man at liberty; he would soon come to grief.

In the strife that now exists, and is hereafter to prevail for the long traffic, no road can hold a share of it a day beyond the time it is, in every respect, as free to compete for it as its rival lines.

Fix the price on any line for a month and the rest of the lines will put their rates down three or five cents a hundred and take the whole of the long traffic for the last twenty-nine days of that month.

In this matter it seems to me that the interests of the company, and of its local patrons, are the same; there can no possible harm result to the local patrons from any rate yielding a profit at which the long business may be done, but rather good in proportion to the profit obtained upon it.

Nothing can be clearer than that the New York roads could not keep their local charges as low as they now are, should they lose the through business. They would assuredly lose it at a higher rate of charge, for it must be evident that being carried, as it is obliged to be carried, at a low figure, yet it is the highest that can be obtained.

The companies would be false to the interest of their local traffic, as well as to the State and city of New York, if they did not strive to procure the largest attainable share of the foreign traffic, however low the rate, upon which any profit whatever can be realized.

The foregoing considerations lead to the following general results:

1st. The increase of railroads throughout the whole West has been so great that every part of that region, which was once solely tributary to New York, has now several avenues to other and rival markets.

2d. The number and character of the new outlets from the West decide by the natural laws of trade what goods shall go by canal and what by more expeditious routes, and no power rests with the State of New York, or her railroads, to change it, and any abridgment of the freedom or ability of the New York railroads to compete for the long business will only throw that business upon other lines and send it to other markets.

3d. The cities lying to the south of New York, having just been brought as near to all, and much nearer to large portions of the West than New York, the prosperity of the latter city requires that the railroads of New York should carry the long business at the lowest possible rates of charge consistent with their being kept in a requisite state of efficiency.

4th. But about two-thirds of the operating expenses are directly increased with the increase of business, and therefore the cost properly to be estimated against new business, which has other outlets as rivals to the road, is but about two-thirds the average cost of the whole, and thus it is fair to estimate that a profit may be obtained on such business, though the price received for it be only equal to the average cost of the whole; but if the local business be done at the same rate it is clear that the entire capital of the company would be lost.

5th. All that portion of the State drained by the road, and to the city of New York, is equally interested with the company in having all the business done upon it which can be procured and which will yield any profit whatever, as it all tends to increase the ability of the company to charge moderate local rates and benefit the State at large by inducing business through its territory.

6th. As the business done against the competition of rival routes, though taken at rates below a fair price, is charged as high as those routes will carry for, the pecuniary advantages rendered to the people who furnish it are far less than those rendered to interior localities, where the railroad charges during much of the year are greatly lower than any other means of transportation, and all through the year it furnishes extensive facilities not otherwise attainable.

7th. The city and State of New York, having just lost their monopoly of the trade of the West, must look to their two great railroads in their effort to retain a fair share of it, and happily in this the interests of the State, fairly understood, are entirely identical with those of the roads.

www.ingramcontent.com/pod-product-compliance
Lightning Source LLC
LaVergne TN
LVHW011142110826
845150LV00008B/2464
* 9 7 8 1 4 1 8 1 9 3 2 7 0 *